FABER NEW POET

Sam Buchan-Watts

——

ff

FABER & FABER

First published in 2016
by Faber & Faber Ltd
Bloomsbury House
74–77 Great Russell Street
London WC1B 3DA

Typeset by Hamish Ironside
Printed in England by Abbeystar

ACKNOWLEDGEMENTS

Thanks are due to the editors of the following publications
where some of these poems first appeared: *Ambit, The Best British
Poetry 2013* and *2015, Lighthouse, Likestarlings, Poetry London,*
newwriting.net. The first line of 'Narrow Contact Zone' is a quote from
Frank O'Hara's 'A Step Away from Them'. 'The Days Go Just Like That'
is indebted to Frances Leviston's 'Humbles'. Thanks to Rachael Allen,
Kit Buchan, Sophie Collins, Andrew Parkes, Olly Todd and Jack
Underwood; to Thomas Karshan and Denise Riley at UEA;
and to my family and friends.

A CIP record for this book
is available from the British Library

ISBN 978-0-571-33041-6

2 4 6 8 10 9 7 5 3 1

Contents

Matters Concerning God

We kept you at arm's reach like a lit birthday cake.
I never saw your fury or your drunk face.
Now the only matter I can picture
is opaque: the soft pink bellow of sun in your ears.

'Are you not jealous of other people's things – on the bus
ride home, of their cars?' There was your calm rebuff,
but that didn't matter. I still keep
the view of your kitchen from the porch,

the hot, halogen hall, your father's chide over grades
from offstage, the way the lamps upstairs unite.
Then the dingy corners, ancient filth and other matter;
places the skylight cannot reach. Maybe that's where you prayed.

Narrow Contact Zone

neon in daylight is a great pleasure

but neon at night is Cineworld, Ashford
lurid, evangelical; cars appear moth-like

within borders of street lamps, merge beneath a sodium fuzz
born of the Pfizer district (*good health is vital to all of us*)

you'd need access through a membrane to switch them off
and the scrapes of grey cloud hunker down

as instructive as discs, and the rows of parapatric shrub
and the loom of junction after junction

the buttressed leisure centre, its bashed signage, and the bonk
of a car's underside over a turfed-up speed bump

the constant half-term limbo, another public holiday on the horizon
the weird mean welcome, *hello ceiling of lights, hello endless space
    to park*

what stillness happens when the movie shows
what type of wind blows

I could save a confession till the credits roll
never quite manage to sit them out till close

The Bridge

I dreamt that we made an unbreakable vow with the bridge, and that we were naive and not au fait with the extent of its vice-like structure (dreams rarely allow for this kind of foresight and, now I come to think of it, weren't the contractors a little rushed, does that side of the bridge not bow a little while the other dominates?) And I have since broken that vow over so many mornings when the weather was stupid and it felt like the city was gearing up for a giant sneeze and in crossing the bridge I didn't own up to feeling uncertain: I carried on cycling, letting the feeling lie latent, like the glycerine moss that looks painted onto the bottom of the bridge supports each time the waves peel back, assuming the feeling would recede like a siren into the distance

And we are both guilty of assuming the bridge and its two views were unassailable and broader than reality; neither one of us attempting to hold that view in our minds so that we could refer back to it later. I regret the many potholes in the road, each with a downwards view of the water, and how I freewheeled on through an air moody with bugs, assuming always that you'd be there to meet me on the other side, a point at which we can take in both views. Not like here, amidst the ruins of our vow, by the riverbank with the snarky remains of a fire, its shadow insisting on the walls and the sight of the wave's urge – like a recurring siren – to overwrite itself once more, just once more again

Moon

We were at an age to go looking for relief in the moon, fanatic about the men we had elected stealing their way through the atmosphere to land on its powdery top, speculating about whether it was brittle like old soap and if it would accommodate their impact. And when the men spoke on the moon, words like 'nation' and 'flag' hit the insides of their glass helmets and bounced back like tennis balls, leaving teeny pockmarks in the five o'clock shadow of their skin. The angles of shadow on their visors were, on reflection, nonsensical. Yet still we speculated about the men's health and not about how the roundness of their helmets is like our idea of the moon, that helmets and the moon are kindred spirits

And how the flag kept flying there at full mast as we resumed our sliding and postured lives, like something profane and unforgettable said to us in our youth, with the far-off persistence a windsock has in its baggy flutter. How lazy we were as a nation not to deviate from the image of a flag we had ready-made, just whipping out the archetypal square-in-a-circle print, and not thinking about our age in relation to the moon, or how everything is in motion except the moon, or in spite of it (as when you turn a saucepan round the egg will keep positing itself the same way inside), or the futility of flags and their fluttering, or of wind or light in the right kind of atmosphere (and this series of thoughts I let go like a spinning top)

Nose to Tail

in places far from here, and colder –
like the northern US states of Wisconsin or Alaska –
pigs can freeze to the sides of trucks or have
their limbs crushed by other pigs' limbs

At a gridlock somewhere in north Norfolk
a two-tier truck of livestock waits next to a school bus.
The spotted pigs in the upper tier could be oinking
the most enormous racket, but the bus is icy private
like a coolbox, and from the top deck all you can do
is glance through the slit where the angle makes
the dark pale and mottled rug of upright pigs
inside have no apparent end. In fact,
it is quite difficult to know exactly where one pig stops
and another begins, and the shape of other pigs
in the lattice of pink flesh
make each individual pig's expression seem a smirk
at being privy to this sequestered mass,
chuffed with the pure occasion of it.

Study of two lamps and a painting

I

Still on at the back of the house, this night light painted
like a prairie shack with a mouse peering round the side.
The enamel isn't chipped, but it has no back –
for a change of bulb – which in the dark appears
to be hacked off, or blown out. It's not the kind of light
you can read by. Someone forgot to turn it off at the wall
so the glow continues to spill like an ache through a tooth,
or the way the musk of a bonfire sieves into a jumper and linge
though the room or house it's in can no longer be pictured.

II

A hall lamp mistakenly read as a home life
from the end of the drive by someone else's dad,
returning the boy home from a birthday party.
It has the worry-glow of a bonfire seen in the distance
through trees, or an ache felt as an ore in tooth enamel.
There is no one around for miles –
it's a catholic kind of black. Stranded then, the boy
bangs and bangs until his hand goes through the window,
hotly dishevelling the kitchen's uncooked dark.

There's a painting of a house in the family, but the memory
has been bleached almost entirely.
It always gets propped up midway down the kitchen table
after certain dinners, and the flick up of the dimmer switch.
The painter, who by this point could do very little but gesture
in acrylics, has pulled the light of the sky
through every square window of the painted square house –
the gleaming acrylic off-white, which reads like a smoke stain
or a tint of enamel – with a dull permanent bright.
A kind of muted explosion that aches on through.

The Plastic Sacks

A new dilemma is nesting in our homes, the kitchens,
   living rooms.
It will make us clamber like lobsters in the dark, boil our
   shoes and eat them.

We keep stashing sacks in networks of sacks,
hyperbreeding to the humming gyrate
of my fridge. Now there are stacks,
and that sterile whiff when you nearly asphyxiate,

in the crevice between dishwasher and chipboard unit.
Magicked to hover there, just above the floor's chill,
where other increments of us sit,
dust, dead flies, dandruff – the homely filth.

They rest without tension, raised a smidgen
like the gossamer fur of soya beans,
a sleep shirt slipping from a girl's chest;
ominous as B-movie graveyard mist.

Car Game Logic

For every statue we erect we eviscerate space: for each road
pinned down some meaningful utterance is snatched like a
fly from a room, marquee tent or empty pool, slimy wet
around the edges. The mole pays back for the molehill: you
can't push matter out or to the side of a dream in a manner
so slipshod. Whatever has come to be required is done or
made regularly, at no small cost. That air freshener is
erected at a lewd angle from the dashboard and cooks its
bleach-cold aroma: it costs the air a bomb. For all the mod
con sound proof there is a whoosh, or hiss, like at any
moment dry ice will creep out over dusty rocks in the
reptile room. I ran short of things to ask my parents in a
manner that suits them while making droplets jump the
landmarks of the school run; to those we owe the
awkwardness. Maybe soon we'll pass Stonehenge, or the
Angel of the North (if one or both didn't only pop up willy-
nilly, if the map knew how to mark them), or the
Eurotunnel drill mounted at some point further along, just
beyond those hills, you're sure (*whatever has come to be
required is done or made regularly, at great cost*, like dry
ice in the reptile room). But the fields are bereft of things,
even trees; perhaps these sights were snatched like a fly
from a room while the hush had become an argument; and
it's not until we quiet again that we clock the car we're in is
not in fact the thing we thought was moving.

'The Days Go Just Like That'

If you emerge from the glove of woods –
the trail's patchiness like jaundiced spliff paper
and the dry powder bloom of a fire extinguisher
let off by kids last night –
blinking, feeling skew-whiff, confused, to find this:
a medieval re-enactment *in medias res*,
then you have seen it exactly as it should be seen:
exposed but distant, so that the quirks –
the radiant tinkle, the gathers of enthusiasts,
the rhubarb-rhubarbs, the unintelligible frills,
the coarseness of sound their makeshift dress makes
like brown paper crumpling as it's being burnt –
are so correct, as if history were a thing to be administered
amidst the afternoon. And the hold-all blue
seems about to decompress, until all we have left
is a far-off clobber of wood. And the days go just like that.

The Days Just Go Like That

Once you resubmerge tipsy and lightly bereft,
cursing your way backwards
into a haze that's styled by trees, you may feel
like an arm retreating into an unwelcoming sleeve,
and realise that the woods cannot smother without an opening
or the roaming shadow of the sun, which stops undulating at the pathway.
You try to hold the re-enacted scene in your mind for as long as possible
but now you are out of it, the dream of medieval jousting is just that:
  a smattering, and the turf track is quickening,
along with the remnants of hash resin
and benzedrine, and filaments of rubber, and the way it all slides
across the muted colour cones of your eyes,
and the clomping of your feet is almost separate
and singular, as the insides of a fire extinguisher –
emptied of its starch and fibre – still retain a fundamental structure,
and there's a city down here somewhere.

The Dogs

My most cherished photographs
transformed overnight into those of dogs:
big horny dogs in their ripest years
hogging the frame for themselves.

Every last photographer's trick employed
so that even in the tacky studio where he couldn't focus
my dog, like a good dog, looks ever curious and propositional
baring his hunk of incisor at us, its nourished decay.

In the more rough-cut alfresco shots with an arty contrast
between negative and positive textures, my black dog
merges with the dark or slides into a pond in such a way
that dog and pond are seamless.

In this dog world one ear of my dog is serendipitously
folded back forever, fixed there,
and though the tawny insides appear knobby and esoteric
they indicate a constant alertness to any thrown ball

or that he is newly ruffled from rolling in the buzzing grass.
There is a choice photo stashed in my wallet,
its creased folds powdery with friction; his profile
is divine against a backdrop of swirling marble blue.

This day I recall for its stressful hilarity; we could not bundle
his legs onto the stool. Since then the dog has been as mute
as the pictures. Perhaps somewhere
in his cropped-out lower throat, his bark is stuck.

Cowcium

What bivalve mollusc has lodged itself within the seafood medley
just served, that needs to be sent back, that makes the room turn,
  sliding
a grey sludge. What nook of the seabed has been disturbed so
  haphazardly
I could almost hear the thing confide were it not for the hot steam,
  and I picture
its drunk lips going squeamish in the company of a battered prawn
  or squid ring
and so it tugs at the pork base of my spine. Were I to squat and have
  someone burrow
with a pair of tweezers newly sterilised with a flame, would they find
  a wedge of guilt,
shaped something like a bivalve mollusc, between the bottom vertebra
and the cubby hole of my pelvis. Could I dry it on the sill in a hot sun
  till it crumbles,
then flake it into the restaurant fish tank where clownfish are
  preoccupied
avoiding the lurid mini castle and the cropped tree root, which
  embarrass them, I conjecture,
more so than the firecracker crustaceans being guzzled to their right.
  I want to watch
their mouths pucker like an arse to the water's skim, and feel
  responsible as a cool, clean knife
cracking open an oyster shell, and talk to them about the cows out
  in the fields,
who brew a thing called milk for our consumption, who sag just to
  make it,
and of the small cows who are calves and are known to drink it as
  well. Milk being
cool, clean liquid which holds our bones and stuff together more
  cheaply than water.

The Word Pavilion

We woke feeling most baffled
by the removal of things: what is
left out for a damp autumn to rot?
The pavilion is thin and unable to fend
for itself. The suburb hasn't room
for its shabby opulence – delicate
as a dried wasp caught on the sill.

The boy runs out into the garden and marks
in chalk a rhomboidal grid where he imagines
the pavilion might have been. What use in
the remark 'autumn is coming' when the roof
isn't there to catch it? The word 'pavilion'
dismantles when he goes to use it
like an old washing peg. The phrase 'a chance of rain'
might go in its place; but the weather changes.

The Loop

I dreamt of the Centre, the distant clatter and growl of activity at the ends of its lifelong halls – halls men were afraid to walk down. One man slipped clownishly on a spill of milk in the waiting room; he didn't allow for its consistency, thicker than water. The tannoy played a clawing baby cry on loop, beneath which the men struggled to be reposed as they leant against vending machines humming modestly. The thought occurred that baby wails are unpleasant because they have to be, otherwise a baby could die, even in a beige and cropped society such as ours, untended. A squeaky toy rolled continuously beneath the chairs nudging men's feet – nobody willing to reach down and pick it up, each the most keen to make himself heard. Each feeling nearly pregnant with a notion of love and becoming, but wanting a tactile space between the cries, stark, like an idea, from their trousers to their lips, saying this noise needs to stop, please, somebody stop this noise

Milestone

The tank of my saloon car had been leaking pale lava which was creeping over the gas station forecourt forming a snug little lake, during the time in which I had opted to satisfy an extra fancy and go back to the counter for a bar of chocolate. The gas station was as it should have been: the correct ratio of ashen chewing gum to wandering shrub; crap salads greeting us from an open fridge Together we – I mean, the other patrons and I – had been waiting for the clerk's manager, Karen, who was busy out in the rear with something and would be with us in one moment, though, looking back it does not seem feasible that the build behind the cigarette cabinet was deep enough for anything like a room with mismatched cardboard boxes or a utilities cupboard with nothing but a wobble-prone plastic school chair and a length of old rope frayed at its ends, lying loose on the floor. The clerk was eager to defer responsibility for our question, and I did not have him down as the lying type, though it was a small, common matter – *we just said that we want an affirmation of character, filling the tanks has made us empty* – and this was long before we ever had the lava to distract us. I thought of my long journey to this point, and to be immodest, exactly how far I'd come in myself (extremely far). That flickering strip of open fields which could puncture the spirit of even the most ardent wayfarer, where piece of grit had lodged itself on the back of my eyeball so that I saw a cordite island with every blink; a hypnagogic destination in each one of these moments. And before I arrived here occurred to me how every gas station out in the sticks has its own moon in daylight; a moon that mocks it from a vantage point where now I sit like a nodding dog

Happens Again
for Wallace Stevens

It was when Bazil said,
'My déjà vu gets so bad I sometimes throw up,'
That the room got brighter.
The TV went off with a blip.

I . . . I think I said,
'Was the TV just on a second ago?'
The static fretted for some time before or after.
We were two figures in the room,

There was a reasonable amount of glare.
'That's a snag in your brain or your gut, not elsewhere.'
The walls begin slotting into the floors, as usual.
The smell of sick is unforgettable.